Kristen Stewart

By Robin Joh

Crabtree Publishing Company

www.crabtreebooks.com

Crabtree Publishing Company
www.crabtreebooks.com

Author: Robin Johnson
Publishing plan research and development:
  Sean Charlebois, Reagan Miller
  Crabtree Publishing Company
Project coordinator: Kathy Middleton
Photo research: Crystal Sikkens
Editors: Molly Aloian, Crystal Sikkens
Proofreader and Indexer: Wendy Scavuzzo
Designer: Ken Wright
Production coordinator and Prepress technician: Ken Wright

Every effort has been made to trace copyright holders and to obtain their permission for use of copyright material. The authors and publishers would be pleased to rectify any error or omission in future editions. All the Internet addresses given in this book were correct at the time of going to press. The author and publishers regret any inconvenience caused if addresses have changed or sites have ceased to exist, but can accept no responsibility for any such changes.

Photographs:
Alamy: © Moviestore Collection Ltd.: page 8; Photos 12: page 9
Associated Press: cover, page 5
Getty Images: Richard Corkery/NY Daily News Archive: page 6; WireImage: page 7
Keystone Press: © Leo Rigah/Starlitepics: page 4; © Paul Fenton/zumapress: page 10; © Sharkpixs/zumapress: pages 12, 27; © ADC: page 13; © BIG Pictures UK: page 14; © VPC/wenn.com: page 15; © Summit Entertainment: pages 16, 23, 24; © Virginia Farneti/zumapress: page 17; © Alex J Berliner/BEImages: page 18; © Sidney Kimmel Entertainment: page 20; © Alec Michael/zumapress: page 21; © Imprint Entertainment: page 22; © River Road Entertainment: page 26
Retna Pictures: Gilbert Flores/CPA: pages 11, 25
Shutterstock: pages 1, 19, 28

Library and Archives Canada Cataloguing in Publication

Johnson, Robin (Robin R.)
  Kristen Stewart / Robin Johnson.

(Superstars!)
Includes index.
Issued also in an electronic format.
ISBN 978-0-7787-7248-4 (bound).--ISBN 978-0-7787-7257-6 (pbk.)

  1. Stewart, Kristen, 1990- --Juvenile literature. 2. Actors--United States--Biography--Juvenile literature. I. Title. II. Series: Superstars! (St. Catharines, Ont.)

PN2287.S685J64 2011   j791.4302'8092   C2010-905311-7

Library of Congress Cataloging-in-Publication Data

Johnson, Robin (Robin R.)
  Kristen Stewart / by Robin Johnson.
    p. cm. -- (Superstars!)
  Includes index.
  ISBN 978-0-7787-7257-6 (pbk. : alk. paper) --
  ISBN 978-0-7787-7248-4 (reinforced library binding : alk. paper) --
  ISBN 978-1-4271-9553-1 (electronic (pdf))
  1. Stewart, Kristen, 1990---Juvenile literature. 2. Actors--United States--Biography--Juvenile literature. I. Title.
  PN2287.S685J64 2010
  791.4302'8092--dc22
  [B]
                                        2010032495

Crabtree Publishing Company
www.crabtreebooks.com   1-800-387-7650

Printed in the USA/102010/SP20100915

Published in Canada
Crabtree Publishing
616 Welland Ave.
St. Catharines, ON
L2M 5V6

Published in the United States
Crabtree Publishing
PMB 59051
350 Fifth Avenue, 59th Floor
New York, New York 10118

Published in the United Kingdom
Crabtree Publishing
Maritime House
Basin Road North, Hove
BN41 1WR

Published in Australia
Crabtree Publishing
386 Mt. Alexander Rd.
Ascot Vale (Melbourne)
VIC 3032

CONTENTS

Words that are defined in the glossary are in
bold type the first time they appear in the text.

A Shooting Star

Kristen Stewart may be the most envied woman in Hollywood. She is a talented young actress who has already been honored with several awards. She is famous, gorgeous, popular, and rich. All that pales in comparison, however, to the one fact that keeps jealous teenage girls up at night— Kristen was cast as Bella Swan in the hit Twilight movies.

Meet Kristen

Kristen has been acting in feature films for more than half of her young life. She has had both lead and supporting roles in a variety of movies from different **genres**. She has appeared in several hit films, including *Panic Room*, *The Messengers*, *In the Land of Women*, and *Into the Wild*.

Award Season

Kristen has been recognized for her work in several feature films. She was nominated for four Young Artist Awards and a People's Choice Award for her acting. She won the Teen Choice and MTV Movie Awards for her starring role in *Twilight*. She even won awards for Best Movie Kiss! Kristen has the pleasure of sharing those awards with handsome *Twilight* co-star Robert Pattinson.

Kristen Stewart and Robert Pattinson accept their second Best Kiss award at the 2010 MTV Movie Awards.

Into the Light

Kristen stepped into the international spotlight when she starred as Bella Swan in the 2008 mega-hit movie *Twilight*. In the film, Bella has a dangerous romance with the ultimate bad boy—a bloodthirsty vampire. A vampire is a fictional creature that rises from the grave to drink the blood of living things. *Twilight* was wildly popular around the world. The film's stars—including the **mortal** Kristen Stewart— became overnight celebrities.

Howl at the Moon

Kristen returned as lovestruck Bella Swan in *The Twilight Saga: New Moon* and *The Twilight Saga: Eclipse*. The hit sequels played in sold-out theaters around the world. The vampire romance series continues to capture the hearts of preteens and teens—and continues to raise the star status of Kristen Stewart.

In the Land of Kristen

Kristen first appeared on the big screen when she was just nine years old. Since then, she has acted in more than 20 films. Kristen has starred in thrillers, dramas, and science-fiction adventure movies. She has played a child bank robber, a teenage abuse victim, and a hippie singer. She has flown through space, hidden from burglars, and run from ghosts. And the fearless actress shows no sign of slowing down.

Kristen at age nine

In Her Blood

Kristen Jaymes Stewart was born on April 9, 1990, in Los Angeles, California. She grew up in the L.A. community of Woodland Hills ("The Valley") with her parents and three brothers Cameron, Dana, and Taylor. Dana and Taylor are Kristen's adopted brothers. Kristen's parents both work in the entertainment industry. Her father, John, is a television producer and stage manager. Her mother Jules is a script supervisor.

A Christmas Miracle

Kristen was "discovered" when she was eight years old. She was acting in her elementary school's Christmas play at the time. Her performance caught the attention of an **agent** who was in the audience. Kristen soon landed her first acting job. She had a non-speaking part—as a girl waiting for a drink—in the children's film *The Thirteenth Year*. Although her role in the film was small, it may have given Kristen a thirst for acting.

She Said It

"To be honest, I had fun at first. It was the first thing I ever thrived at. My parents are crew. They were both baffled that I wanted to act. But they support anything that [I] want to do. It was something I thought was fun because I grew up on sets."
—Discussing the start of her acting career in *Interview* magazine, October 2009

School Is Out

Kristen stopped attending public school when she was in the seventh grade. The busy actress continued to study by **correspondence**, however. Kristen recently graduated from high school with honors. She hopes to continue her education by attending college.

Panic Attack

After a series of minor movie roles—including a part in the **independent** drama *The Safety of Objects*—Kristen got her first big break. In 2002, she starred with Jodie Foster in the thriller *Panic Room*. In the film, Kristen's character must hide with her mother in a safe room to avoid gun-toting burglars. Kristen had no need to panic, however. Both the film and her performance in it were praised by viewers and critics around the world. Her success in *Panic Room* opened new doors for the up-and-coming actress.

Kristen and Jodie Foster were both nominated for awards for their performances in *Panic Room*.

A Lucky Break

Nicole Kidman and Hayden Panettiere were originally cast to star as mother and daughter in *Panic Room*. Nicole was injured while making another movie and was forced to drop out of the film, however. Jodie Foster was cast in her place. Kristen was hired to replace Hayden in the film because she looked more like Jodie.

Catch That Girl

Kristen's breakout performance in *Panic Room* earned her roles in a variety of feature films over the next few years. In the R-rated thrillers *Cold Creek Manor* and *Undertow*, Kristen's supporting roles gave adults something to scream about. In the action film *Catch That Kid*, her bank-robbing character stole the hearts of young viewers. Kristen even captured the attention of Zorgons! Zorgons are aliens in the fantasy-adventure film *Zathura*. Kristen co-starred in the film as a teenager who was trapped in her house with her two bickering brothers while the house was magically hurtling through space.

Corbin Bleu (left) and Max Thieriot (right) starred with Kristen in *Catch That Kid*.

Speak No Evil

When she was 13 years old, Kristen starred in the independent movie *Speak*. In the film, she played the part of Melinda Sordino, a high school freshman who was abused by an older student. Melinda stopped speaking to her family and friends as she coped with her overwhelming pain. Kristen's powerful performance in the film left audiences speechless, too. *Speak* earned her a reputation as a talented young actress. It also led to her real-life romance with her co-star, American actor Michael Angarano.

Shooting the Messengers

In 2007, Kristen starred in the supernatural thriller *The Messengers*. In the film, she played the lead character Jess Solomon. Jess was tormented and attacked by ghosts on her family's haunted sunflower farm. The creepy PG-rated movie was popular with young audiences. Kristen's strong performance couldn't save the film from horrifying reviews, however.

Drama Queen

Kristen's movie career took a dramatic turn later that year. She starred in the dramas *In the Land of Women* and *The Cake Eaters*. She also had a supporting role in the hit movie *Into the Wild*. *Into the Wild* is a dramatic tale of one man's effort to find the meaning of life in the Alaskan wilderness. Critics were wild about Kristen's performance as a hippie singer in the Oscar-nominated film.

The Hollywood Premiere of *Into the Wild* was held at the DGA Theater in California.

Style File

Although Kristen often walks the red carpet, she prefers to walk in Converse sneakers. The petite actress—she is 5 feet 5 inches (1.65 m) tall—wears "anything that's beat up." In an interview in *Vanity Fair* magazine, she admits "I kind of like to look like a hobo."

Kristen walks the red carpet in Converse sneakers at the 2009 MTV Movie Awards.

What Just Happened?

In 2008, Kristen appeared in the films *Jumper* and *The Yellow Handkerchief.* She also had a supporting role in the independent movie *What Just Happened*? In the film, she played Zoe, the teen daughter of a Hollywood producer. With an all-star cast that included Robert De Niro, Sean Penn, and Bruce Willis, *What Just Happened*? helped earn Kristen a spot on Hollywood's A-list. However, no movie had a more dramatic effect on Kristen's career that year than the mega-hit *Twilight.*

The Bella of the Ball

On November 21, 2008, the romantic fantasy film *Twilight* flew into theaters. The movie was an instant success, making close to $36 million its first day! The film transformed Kristen Stewart into an international superstar. It also made her the envy of millions of vampire-crazy girls around the world.

Fans line up to get autographs from Kristen as she arrives at the *Late Show with David Letterman* studio on November 20, 2008.

Kiss of Death

Twilight is the tale of a girl and a vampire who fall dangerously in love. Their romance begins when Bella moves to Forks, Washington, and meets Edward (played by British actor Robert Pattinson). She is intrigued by the mysterious, darkly handsome boy in her biology class. Bella later discovers the horrifying truth about her bloodthirsty crush. By then, Bella has already fallen deeply in love with Edward. Their relationship—and its deadly complications—are the basis of both the film and the wildly popular *Twilight* book on which it is based.

Kristen and Robert captivate audiences in the movie *Twilight*.

She Said It

"I thought it was really ambitious, this portrayal of the ultimate, most epic love story that could be. Also, Bella is not a typical female lead. The power balance between her and Edward is really skewed. Edward is this confident, perfect, **idealistic** man, although deep down he's actually really afraid. Bella is naïve but also sure-footed. Whatever it is inside of her that drives her is stronger than she is. She just trusts…herself."
—Describing her first impression of *Twilight* in *Vanity Fair*, November 2008

The *Twilight* Phenomenon

The film *Twilight* is based on the bestselling novel by Stephenie Meyer. It is the first book in a series of vampire romance novels written for preteens and teens. *Twilight* hit book stores in October 2005 and, by August 2008, the last book of the series had been released. These books had become so popular, when the first book hit the big screen in November 2008, the series had become a cultural **phenomenon**. Twi-hards lined the streets and crowded into theaters for the opening of the *Twilight* movie and its sequels *The Twilight Saga: New Moon* and *The Twilight Saga: Eclipse*. Nothing could stop devoted fans from being the first to see their favorite love story come alive.

DIE-HARD TWI-HARDS

Twi-hards, Twilighters, or fanpires are the most **devoted** fans of the *Twilight* series. They have strong opinions about every aspect of the popular books and movies—and are not afraid to share them!

Fans camped out for three days before the premiere of *The Twilight Saga: Eclipse.*

She Said It

"*Usually, what drives you is your own personal responsibility to the script and the character and the people you are working with. But in this case, I have a responsibility not only to that but to everyone who has personal involvement in the books—and now that spans the world.*"
—Discussing the *Twilight* phenomenon in *Interview* magazine, October 2009

Brown-Eyed Girl

Kristen plays the role of Bella in *The Twilight Saga* movies. Isabella "Bella" Marie Swan is a sweet, shy, 17-year-old girl. She has a heart-shaped face, fair skin, long brown hair, and chocolate-brown eyes. She is extremely clumsy and bites her fingernails when she is nervous. In the *Twilight* book, Edward describes Bella as "the opposite of ordinary" and "much more than beautiful." Bella will do anything to keep her romance with Edward alive—even if it kills her.

DON'T GO CHANGING

Kristen has naturally blonde hair and green eyes. She had to dye her hair brown and wear brown contact lenses when playing the role of Bella.

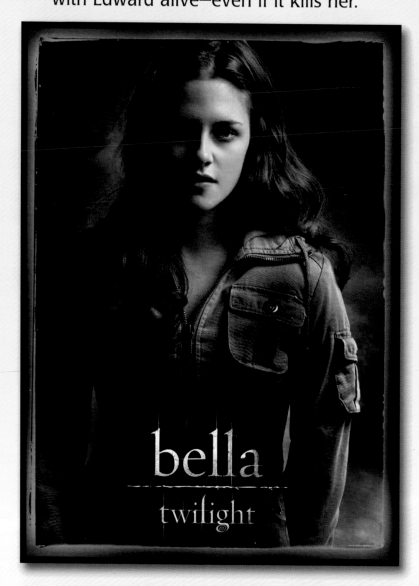

bella

twilight

16

Sort of Perfect

Kristen landed the role of Bella after a four-hour audition with *Twilight* director Catherine Hardwicke. Kristen then helped cast the role of Edward Cullen. After a day of auditions and a parade of leading men, she told the director that Robert Pattinson was the obvious choice for the role. Kristen later told *Vanity Fair* magazine that casting Robert "couldn't have been better. It was sort of perfect."

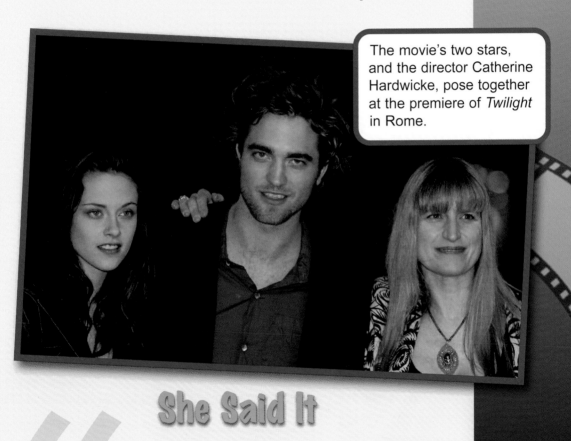

The movie's two stars, and the director Catherine Hardwicke, pose together at the premiere of *Twilight* in Rome.

She Said It

"*I'm very excited to have Kristen Stewart play Bella in the upcoming* Twilight *movie. She's an amazing actress with experience all across the board—action, horror, comedy, romance, and more. Since* Twilight *has moments that fit into every one of these genres, I'm thrilled to have a Bella who has practice with them all.*"
—*Twilight* author Stephenie Meyer, discussing the casting of Kristen Stewart on StephenieMeyer.com, November 2007

17

Casting Call

Stephenie Meyer's first choice for the role of Bella Swan was Australian actress Emily Browning. Emily did not audition for the part, however. She was too tired from filming *The Uninvited* to consider making a trilogy. Other fan favorites for the role included Alexis Bledel, Rachel McAdams, and Anna Paquin. Most Twi-hards now accept Kristen as their beloved Bella. The popular actress is swarmed by adoring fans wherever she goes!

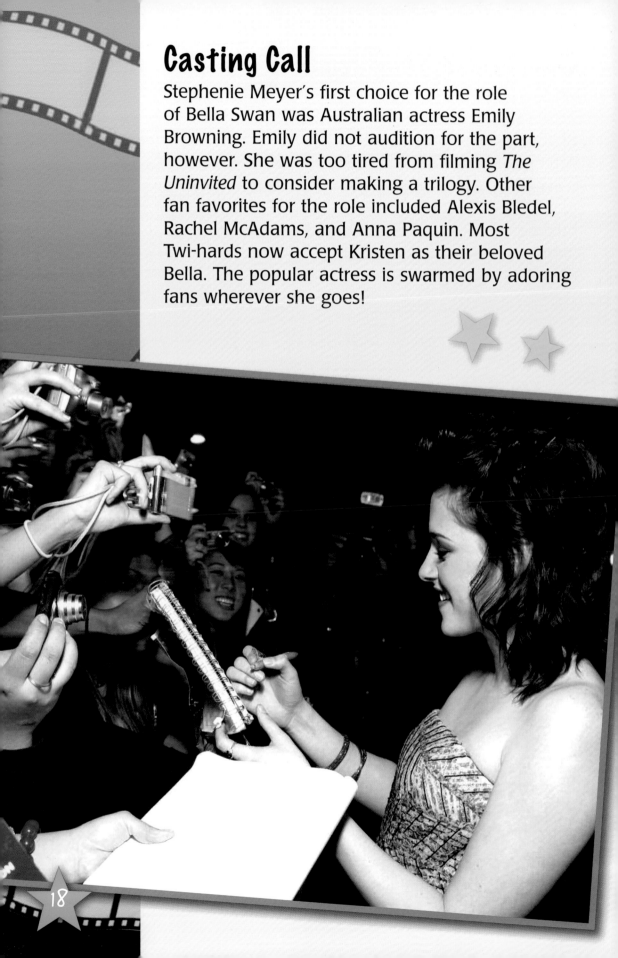

Beauty and the Beast

Kristen and Robert are rumored to be dating. The young stars have a powerful connection both on screen and off. Catherine Hardwicke described the couple's first audition together—a bedroom scene at her house—as "electric." Stephenie Meyer warned moviegoers that Kristen and Robert's "on-screen chemistry may cause **hyperventilation**."

Robert Pattinson and Kristen Stewart

He Said It

"When I met Kristen, there was instant chemistry. She brought something out of me that I can't even explain."
—Robert Pattinson, in *Teen Vogue* magazine, November 2008

The Adventure Continues

Kristen continues to light up the big screen. She recently starred in *New Moon* and *Eclipse*, the hit sequels to *Twilight*. She also appeared in several films that were noticeably lacking the **undead**.

Fun and Games

In 2009, Kristen continued her movie-making adventure with the quirky film *Adventureland*. In the film, she stars as a rich college student who works at an amusement park for fun. Her character has even more fun when she begins a romance with a co-worker. The film received positive reviews but was not widely shown in theaters.

New Moon Rising

The sequel to *Twilight*, on the other hand, played to sold-out crowds around the world. *The Twilight Saga: New Moon* opened on November 20, 2009. It shattered attendance records, earning more than $72 million in Canada and the United States that day! Twi-hards lined up days before the premiere to see the big-budget special effects and big-screen love triangle. Kristen **reprised** her role as the hauntingly beautiful Bella Swan in the mega-hit movie.

TRIPLE CROWN

The stars of the Twilight series were honored with a 2010 People's Choice Award. Kristen Stewart, Robert Pattinson, and Taylor Lautner won the prize for Favorite On-Screen Team.

Kristen attends the world premiere of *The Twilight Saga: New Moon*.

Dark Side of the Moon

New Moon continues the love story between Bella and Edward. In the film, Edward moves from Forks to protect Bella from his dangerous—and increasingly thirsty—family. Bella longs for Edward but finds comfort in her friendship with werewolf Jacob Black (played by teen idol Taylor Lautner). Bella and Edward are reunited at the end of the film but do not live happily ever after. Edward learns that he must destroy his true love—or change her forever.

WOLF GIRL

Kristen has a real liking for wolves. She owns two pet **hybrid** wolves, a female named Lily and a male named Jack. I guess you can say she has her own real-life "wolf pack"!

In this scene from *The Twilight Saga: New Moon* Jacob saves Bella from drowning.

She Said It

"If you make movies and you don't care about the people who watch, then you probably are just wanting to be rich and famous. The fact that these movies are important to so many people makes me so happy. I care that they care."
—Discussing the Twilight films and fans in Parade.com, November 2009

Worth the Wait

Twi-hards around the world eagerly waited for the opening of the third film in the Twilight series—and most agreed it was worth the wait. *The Twilight Saga: Eclipse*—which again starred Kristen Stewart, Robert Pattinson, and Taylor Lautner—was released on Wednesday, June 30, 2010. It set a box office record for a movie opening on a Wednesday, taking in $68.5 million!

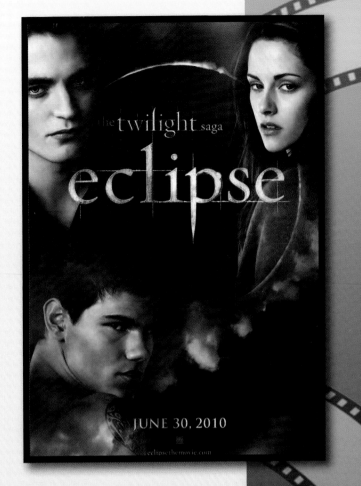

She Said It

"Just as you think you're going to get the same story, all of a sudden it completely changes. Bella is back to herself. She's comfortable and self-assured in a way that she wasn't in New Moon. What I really loved about Eclipse was exploring different levels of love and acknowledging that the ideals that you had aren't totally true. The other thing is that Bella's **innately** honest. But in Eclipse, she lies to herself and she lies to everybody around her, about the fact that she's in love with Jacob. That changes everything."

—Discussing the film *Eclipse* in Parade.com, November 2009

By the Book

The film *The Twilight Saga: Eclipse* is based on Stephenie Meyer's popular novel of the same name. In the movie, the Cullen family unites with Jacob's wolf pack to destroy a group of bloodthirsty vampires. Bella is torn between Edward and Jacob, two very different—but equally gorgeous—creatures.

The Twilight finale is set to begin filming in the fall of 2010. *Breaking Dawn* will be divided into two feature films. Part 1 is scheduled to be released on November 18, 2011, and Part 2 will follow in 2012 on November 16.

Edward aims to keep Bella safe from a **vengeful** vampire in *Eclipse*.

She Said It

"I'm glad to be a part of something that's actually bigger than me for once. The success of it is the coolest thing ever because I can't tell you how much it hurts to do something that you feel like you can really learn from—and you feel is an important section of your life that you put everything into—and then nothing, it just never comes out. So the fact that we can share that, that's why we do this. It's the coolest thing."
—Discussing the success of the Twilight films in *Seventeen* magazine, November 2009

Runaway Success

Kristen also starred in several other films in 2010. In *The Runaways*, Kristen gets groovy as 1970s girl-band rocker Joan Jett. Although Kristen sings and plays guitar in the film, it was not a "runaway" success. In the independent drama *Welcome to the Rileys*, Kristen plays a troubled young girl who connects with a married man. Critics are already welcoming the film, which is scheduled for release in November 2010.

Kristen is pretty in pink at the premiere of *The Runaways*.

Kristen Rocks!

Like her character in *The Runaways*, Kristen is a talented singer and guitar player. She enjoys making music with her friends—including guitar-playing Robert Pattinson. She listens to such bands as The Beatles, The Rolling Stones, and Radiohead. Kristen also likes to write, read books, and watch movies. Her favorite book is John Steinbeck's *East of Eden*. Her favorite films include *The Shining* and *The Jungle Book*.

Kristen shows off her guitar-playing skills in a scene from *The Runaways*.

She Said It

"*I want to go to college for literature. I want to be a writer. I mean, I love what I do, but it's not all I want to do—be a professional liar for the rest of my life.*"
—In an interview for *Vanity Fair*, April 2007

Going on the Road

Kristen will appear in a new movie opening in 2011 called *On the Road*. The movie will be based on the 1957 novel with the same name by Jack Kerouac. The story follows two men as they travel across America. Kristen plays the wife of one of the men. Kristen has also been cast to appear in the drama *K-11*. The film—which will be directed by Kristen's mother Jules Mann-Stewart—studies life in an **eccentric** dormitory of the L.A. County Jail. In the film, Kristen plays an autistic prisoner named Butterfly.

After Twilight

The role of vampire-loving Bella Swan has made Kristen Stewart **immortal**. Her most challenging job now may be to move beyond the *Twilight* phenomenon. Kristen's recent films show her talent and **versatility**—and that there is life for the young actress after the undead.

Timeline

1990: Kristen Jaymes Stewart is born on April 9 in Los Angeles, California.

1999: She lands her first film role in the children's movie *The Thirteenth Year*.

2001: Kristen has a minor role in the independent drama *The Safety of Objects*.

2002: She stars opposite Jodi Foster in the popular thriller *Panic Room*.

2003: She stars in the thriller *Cold Creek Manor*.

2004: Kristen gives a partly speechless performance in the film *Speak*, and stars in the family film *Catch That Kid* and the thriller *Undertow*.

2005: She appears in the fantasy film *Zathura*.

2007: Kristen stars in the films *The Messengers*, *In the Land of Women*, *The Cake Eaters*, and *Into the Wild*.

2008: She co-stars in the dramatic film *The Yellow Handkerchief*, joins the cast of the film *What Just Happened?*, and has a **cameo** in the film *Jumper*.

2008: *Twilight* opens on November 21. Kristen plays vampire-loving Bella Swan in the film.

2009: The adventure continues for Kristen when she stars in the film *Adventureland*.

2009: Kristen returns as Bella Swan on November 20 when *The Twilight Saga: New Moon* opens.

2010: *The Twilight Saga: Eclipse* opens in theaters on June 30. Kristen brings Bella Swan back to life.

2010: Kristen rocks as 1970s girl-band rocker Joan Jett in the film *The Runaways* and stars in the independent drama film *Welcome to the Rileys*.

2010: Kristen is scheduled to star in *K-11*, a film directed by her mother Jules Mann-Stewart.

2010: Kristen begins filming the movie *On the Road*, opening in theaters in 2011.

2010: Kristen will return once more as Bella Swan in the two-part finale of *The Twilight Saga: Breaking Dawn*, opening in 2011 and 2012.

Glossary

agent A person who acts on behalf of someone else

cameo A brief appearance in a film by a well-known actor

correspondence The exchange of school work by mail

devoted Giving much time and attention to a certain cause, activity, or person

eccentric Something that looks different from normal

genres Types or categories of movies or books

hybrid Something that is mixed

hyperventilation Breathing harder and faster than is necessary

idealistic Describing a person who lives by a standard of perfection or beauty

immortal Describing a person or creature who lives forever and cannot die

independent Describing an art movie that is not produced by a large film studio

innately A quality or characteristic that is part of someone or something's nature

phenomenon An extraordinary or unusual event

reprised Repeated a role from a previous movie or play

undead People who have died but act as though they are alive

vengeful Someone or something that is seeking revenge

versatility The ability to do many things well

Find Out More

Books

Orr, Tamra. *Kristen Stewart*. Hockessin, DE:
   Mitchell Lane Publishers, 2010.

Rusher, Josie. *Kristen Stewart: Infinite Romance*.
   London, England: Orion Books, 2009.

Websites

Kristen Stewart
   http://www.kristenstewart.com/
A website that celebrates Kristen's many
achievements

Kristen Stewart Central
   http://k-stewart.net/
A complete online guide to K-Stew

Kristen Stewart Fan
   http://www.kstewartfan.org/
Another fan site devoted to Kristen Stewart

The Twilight Saga
   http://www.thetwilightsaga.com/
The official website for fans *of The Twilight
Saga* books

Index

About the Author

Robin Johnson is a freelance writer and editor. The author of several children's books– including *Ice Hockey and Curling*, *Rodeo*, *Show Jumping*, and *The Mississippi River: America's Mighty River*–she has worked in the publishing industry for more than a decade. When she isn't working, she divides her time between renovating her home with her husband, taking her two sons to hockey practice, and exploring back roads.